In Case Nobody Told You...

Passages of Wisdom and Encouragement

By

Emily Maroutian

In Case Nobody Told You...

Passages of Wisdom and Encouragement

By

Emily Maroutian

ISBN-13: 978-1984927293

First Printing

Printed and bound in the United States of America by Createspace, a division of Amazon.com

empowered by

Maroutian Entertainment
Los Angeles, California
www.maroutian.com

Transformational Books
By Emily Maroutian:

A Second Opinion:
Theories and Observations on Life and Human Behavior

The Process of "I":
An Exploration into the Intertwined Relationship between
Identity and Environment

The Energy of Emotions:
The 10 Emotional Environments and How They Shape the
World Around Us

Thirty:
A Collection of Personal Quotes, Advice, and Lessons

The Empowered Self:
Over 100 Activities and Steps For Creating An Empowered
Mind

The Book of Relief:
Passages and Exercises to Relieve Negative Emotion and
Create More Ease in The Body

Adventures in Thinking:
Opening The Mind Beyond Practiced Limitations

In Case Nobody Told You:
Passages of Wisdom and Encouragement

This Book is a Gift

To:

_____

From:

_____

Date:

_____

I'm gifting you this book because

_____

_____

_____

_____

_____

_____

_____

_____

_____

_____

_____

_____

_____

Note From The Author:

May this book offer you the answers you have been looking for. May it bring relief in your growth and hope about your circumstances. May it bring encouragement about your future and what's possible for you. May you find direction and clarity in how to move forward. May you find peace of mind and an understanding that will help you through tough times. May it be a source of insight when you don't know where to turn. May it continue to provide answers every time you return to it in the future.

If you received this book as a gift, know that the presenter cares deeply about your self-development and wants to see you thrive in life. They are rooting for your success and want to offer you another resource to help you in your journey. In fact, when they read through this book, they thought of you. Not because you needed it, but because they wanted to make sure you have the benefit of clarity, encouragement, and self-assurance. May it take you farther than you ever imagined.

Be you. Be free. Thrive.

Your creativity is your right.

You have a right to sing and dance and write and paint. You are a creative being, and it is nourishing for you to express that creativity in any way it chooses to come out. It doesn't matter if others like it or hate it; it's not about their approval. It's about the stories and feelings within you that need to be released.

You don't necessarily have to make a living at it. You don't have to make money doing it. You don't even have to show it to anyone else. All you have to do is enjoy the process of creating because it comes naturally to you.

Your life is on your timeline.

Your life is not on anyone else's schedule. You're the one who gets to decide what you want and when to pursue it. You decide when you're going to get married, or if you're going to get married at all. You decide when and if you have children. You decide which career you're going to choose, where you're going to live, and how you're going to live.

You might listen to another person's advice from time to time, but at the end of the day, it's your life. You're the one who is going to have to live inside the life you're creating. You're the one who is going to have to wake up every day with the choices you've made. Make sure it's your choice.

Follow your own inner guidance.

At some point, you have to stop needing consensus for your choices. You have to stop needing to justify your right to live your life your way. You don't need other people to give you permission to follow your own intuition. You know what's best for you. You only need to follow your own inner guidance.

Don't let anyone else pressure you into living a life you feel is not for you. Don't allow guilt or any other form of manipulation to throw you off your course. Your life is yours and you should live it the way you feel is right. Give yourself the permission you need to move forward in your own way.

You don't need agreement to be yourself.

Regardless of how much you explain, you will never be able to get the entire world to agree with you. They'll never see you the way you want them to see you, and they'll never respond the way you want them to respond. Regardless of anyone else's beliefs, judgments, or visions of you, you have a responsibility to be yourself. You don't owe anyone agreement on their ideas of who you should be.

You are not defined by how others see you. You are not controlled by how others feel about you. You are not ruled by what others want from you. You have a right to choose your "self" away from what others think about it. No one else decides who you are. You don't owe anyone your freedom of identity.

You deserve a loving and supportive relationship.

You will participate in several different relationships throughout your life. Some will be romantic, some will be familial, and others will be platonic. None of those categories will determine the length, value, or quality of the relationship.

The true worth of the relationship can be determined by how the other person treats you. How do they make you feel? Do you shrink or expand in their presence? Do they see you for who you are and not for who they want you to be? Do they value you? If yes, then, they'll value the relationship they have with you and you'll be able to see it clearly. You won't have to second-guess or question whether they care for you. You'll know by how they treat you.

Don't forget to choose happiness.

In life, you will feel sad, maybe even depressed. You will feel angry and frustrated. You will feel desperate and confused. You will go through every emotion human beings can experience. However, don't forget that you also have a right to feel happiness. You also deserve those moments that make you feel glad you're there to experience them.

You deserve fun nights with good friends and the kind of laughter that leaves your stomach muscles aching for days afterwards. You deserve the kindness of a gentle shoulder and a warm hug from a loving companion. You deserve people who understand you and the feeling of ease radiating throughout your being. You deserve to feel and experience good things, too. So, don't forget to choose happiness every once in a while.

Release the anger, but keep the lesson.

Anger says, "This isn't right." Sometimes that's an accurate assessment, and sometimes it isn't. You won't know for certain until your emotions have shifted. Anger can fog up your mind temporarily and make you blind to the important details of a situation.

Validate the anger, but don't hold onto it. It's usually a symptom of feeling unfairness, so you don't want to dismiss it completely because there's a lesson within it. However, anger can't offer you a workable solution for whatever you're angry about. It can only show you what isn't working for you in that moment. It might not be an accurate evaluation.

To get to a resolution, you have to get past the anger. Then, you'll be able to see whether the anger was accurate and whether something needs to change. Maybe it's you, maybe it's the other person, or maybe it's the situation. You won't be able to see it clearly until you get past the anger.

So, feel what you need to feel. Release what you need to release, but keep the wisdom of the experience. Let it grow you. Let it show you what needs more work. Release the anger, but keep the lesson.

You set the tone for your space.

Everyone tries to carve out a little space for themselves in this big world. A place they can feel safe. A place they can call home. Most people think these spaces are physical, like a giant mansion on top of a hill or a quiet cabin in the woods.

However, most people take their space with them through the energy they carry everywhere they go. Whether they live in the mansion or the cabin, they're the ones who define the space. It's their presence that creates the space, not their possessions or the length of the walls.

Everywhere they go, they'll take their joy or loneliness with them. They'll make that place cool and fun, or drab and depressing. They'll bring their creativity. They'll bring their anger. They lie on their wounds and use their regrets as a bed to sleep in.

Your space is an extension of your inner world. No amount of mansions will fulfill you if your inner space is small, dark, and lonely. Renovate yourself first, and you can be happy anywhere.

You have a right to feel like you belong.

Don't tolerate anyone who makes you feel as if don't belong in this world. They are not your people. They will never see you the way you deserve to be seen and loved. They won't remind you that you are a unique soul who brings light into their lives and makes them feel blessed for getting the chance to know you. They will waste your time, they will take your energy, and they will leave you feeling small. When they do, remember that you are not a burden. Remember that you belong. Just not with them.

When you meet your people, you will feel yourself wake up in their presence. You will be filled with excitement as they activate fun and lightheartedness within you. You'll joke and play and feel cheerful. They will leave you with more energy, not less. They will make you feel heard and seen and loved. They will welcome you into the tribe and make you feel as if you have finally come home.

You have a right to your independence.

Just as you have a right to belong, you also have a right to your independence outside of any tribe, community, or relationship. If it's a healthy environment, they will allow you the space to explore, learn, and grow without being threatened by your need to expand or your need to express something different.

Your identity is only partly defined by a group. Their purpose is not to own you but to offer you support and guidance when you need it. If they truly love you, they'll give you the space to be yourself without guilt, shame, or pressure.

You have to a right to be yourself, to express yourself, to share yourself regardless of what tribe or group you belong to. They exist to make you feel less alone, not more. They exist to make you feel more understood, not less. If they're not serving that purpose, then you need a new tribe.

Set and keep your boundaries.

There are two types of situations in which you might hurt another person's feelings. One is acceptable; the other is not. It is not acceptable to intentionally inflict harm on another person because of the way you're feeling. Your mood does not give you permission to behave poorly.

On the other hand, it is okay to hurt someone's feelings if it occurs while you're setting boundaries, protecting yourself, or participating in self-care. If you choose to stay in because you're exhausted, then you are not intending to hurt your friend when you decline her invitation. You are choosing your own health and wellbeing as opposed to trying to hurt her.

Saying no to others is an acceptable form of hurting their feelings. You will have to do it many times in your life if you want to stay balanced and healthy. You might as well start practicing early.

You can't fail at life.

Failure is simply an unplanned outcome. For the most part, it means you didn't receive the result you wanted. We are all familiar with that occurrence and feeling. However, if you make it mean that you yourself are a failure, then you'll discourage yourself from trying again. You'll keep yourself stuck to avoid painful feelings until eventually being stuck becomes the worst feeling.

We all have different journeys. The only people who feel as though they have failed are the ones comparing their lives with others. Forget the image you have in your mind about how it should all look. Your life is unique to you. Don't try to make it look like anyone else's.

Validate others.

Most people you meet will not care about how much money you make or what kind of car you drive. Most people will care about how you treat them. If you make them feel heard and validated, that feeling will override anything of supposed importance that money can buy. People value your value of them, and there is no price tag on a friend who truly sees you and loves you for who you are.

Don't be afraid to choose the higher path.

Sometimes, life will offer you two hard choices and you won't know which one will work out best for you. You'll weigh the pros and cons, you'll ask for advice from the people you love, and you'll imagine what both roads will look like for you. You'll make up your mind, then you'll change it. You'll feel confused, anxious, and maybe even frustrated.

One path will feel safer than the other, and you'll be tempted to use that as a gauge for your future happiness. But the questions you must ask yourself are, "Who will I become if I take this path? How will this path grow me? Who will it turn me into?" And then finally, "Do I want to be that person?" Choose the path that best aligns with your highest self.

Don't be fair, be you.

When you meet unkind people, you will be tempted to return their treatment. You will want to be fair and mirror their unkindness back to them. Instead of being fair, be you. You are not unkind. You don't have to become what others are, and you don't have to meet people on their level. Be unfair; offer them better.

Unkind people meet unkindness everywhere they go because most people give them the same behavior in return. And so, they meet their own hostile selves reflected within others. This keeps them locked in a cycle, a prison of unkindness they can't break free from. You have the power to interrupt their pattern by offering them something no one else can—yourself.

You own your life.

Your thoughts, feelings, behaviors, desires, dreams, and goals belong to you. You are in charge of you. And when you give that power away to anyone else, you will suffer. Maybe not today, maybe not next week, but there will come a time when you will feel the misalignment of your inner being and your outer life.

Your instincts will tell you to follow your own path, your intuition will call out the right way, your heart will yearn for self-authenticity. And each day you don't listen to it, you'll sink deeper into the depths of disempowerment. Listen to the call, and don't ignore the yearning. You get this one life, and you should live it as you want to live it.

Change takes time and work.

Changing anything in life takes time and commitment. Neither healing nor success happens overnight. The only thing that can change your life in one day is either a trauma or a miracle. Everything else takes time.

So take your time and be easy on yourself as you try to work through your desires and goals. You don't have to figure out your life in one day. You don't have to have the perfect plan tomorrow. You don't have to become a reassembled person in one month.

Sometimes, you just have to take the day as it comes and wait until you feel better to act. Contrary to what others believe, rest and relaxation are a part of the process. Progress doesn't happen without self-care. Being kind to yourself as you are growing will go a long way in helping you change your life for the better.

Develop strong mental habits.

Some people will be smarter than you, some people will be richer than you, and some people will be born in better circumstances, but if you can develop strong mental habits, then you will be at a greater advantage than all of them.

No amount of money can help a person who chooses to remain ignorant. No amount of opportunities can benefit a person who doesn't know how to use them. Your circumstances don't matter as much as how you utilize your mind. People who are successful don't have fewer problems; they've just learned how to be good at finding solutions.

So put your focus and energy in developing your mind, not your bank account. Your mind will lead you to a bigger bank account.

You are the value.

In life, you will have moments when you wonder if you're good enough for a job, another person, or something else that you really want. When you appraise the importance of your desire as being more valuable than yourself, then you are creating an imbalance in your self-perception. You place the significance on the thing that is outside of yourself as opposed to who you are within yourself. This takes away your power and gives it to an external force. The true question is whether the job, relationship, or thing is good enough for you. Does it align with the vision you have for yourself and your life? Is it worthy of your time and energy? Will it better you? Will it fulfill you? Does *it* deserve you?

Keep your mental needs in balance.

Both solitude and community are required for optimum emotional and mental health. You must have equal time to connect with others as well as with yourself. If you have too much of one and not enough of the other, then some aspect of your being will fall into misbalance. Stay connected with yourself and stay connected with others.

It will be mirrored until it is healed.

Anything left unresolved within you will come back to you through other people, situations, and circumstances until it finds completion. If you find yourself going through the same issues or problems time and time again, know that there is some aspect of it you haven't yet healed or released. You will keep pulling it into your experience until you transcend it.

Expose yourself to various experiences.

You grow a little bit through each new experience, even if it seems unimportant at first. The most seemingly mundane task can teach you crucial lessons about life. You can discover the proper application of successful methods through routes you never considered. Even gardening will teach you about patience, space management, growth, and formulas that yield desired results.

Try not to dismiss the wisdom around you simply because it appears trivial. A simple skill in one area can become crucial in another. You won't always recognize the connection, but it's there.

Love is given freely and without condition.

Don't ever believe that your love or devotion is measured by how much pain and suffering you're willing to endure at the hands of friends, family, or lovers. Anyone who truly loves you will not require your wellbeing as sacrifice for their wholeness. You don't have to give yourself to those who take without regard to how it affects you. Your love for others should not drain you dry or make you sick. That's co-dependency. Real love does not need to be earned. It is given freely and without condition.

You are not how others define you.

People who call you derogatory names are not speaking your truth; they are speaking their pain. They can't truly see you because their unhappiness is distorting their view. Their wounds ache in their experience of you because they remain unhealed.

Don't accept their perception of you as your identity. You are more than they are able to see or understand from their position of pain. Don't redefine yourself simply because others haven't done their inner work.

You are stronger than you realize.

Some days, your strength will encourage you to move forward on your own; while on other days, it will nudge you to ask for help from others. Neither is incorrect, and neither is a sign of weakness. If you need to get someone else's advice, support, or help, know that it doesn't diminish your strength. True strength includes an element of wisdom, and wisdom is knowing the difference between when you can do something on your own and when you need assistance.

Choice is power.

Our feelings of freedom and empowerment are proportional to our capacity to choose for ourselves. Self-leadership is the determining factor for our happiness because it allows us to choose who we are, what we want, and which options we're going to pursue.

We feel least free when we feel obligated or restricted in our choices. We feel as though our lives don't belong to us. Then, we feel disempowered and unmotivated to move forward.

Choice is power. The more possibilities we can see for ourselves, the more freedom we feel. Moreover, as we feel more freedom, we feel more powerful. It's important that you feel as though you are choosing your life and not just settling for what others give you.

Every decision you make, choose it as the best option for this moment. Keep doing that until you create better options.

It's better to suffer in reality than in imagination.

Most fear comes from the anticipation of an event rather than the actual event itself. We suffer more when we think about it than when it actually happens. We worry beforehand as a form of preparation because we want to get ahead of our negative predictions so we don't suffer later. It's disguised as mental precaution when it's actually self-inflicted torment. It's a misguided way of minimizing suffering because it only increases it. The price of being ready for future suffering is that you suffer in the present moment. However, if you wait until the event occurs before you worry about it, you'll find that 95% of the time it never even happens.

Speak your truth anyway.

One of the hardest and bravest things you will do is to speak your truth when the voices around you demand agreement. Some people will shout at you, intimidate you, or try to silence you into compliance. This is one of the toughest times for you to use your voice, but it is also the most crucial time for you to speak up.

They'll judge you for it, but you must speak anyway. They'll criticize you personally for your thoughts, but you must be yourself anyway. They'll want you to change into something they can understand, something comfortable, and easy to handle. Be yourself anyway. You didn't come here to sweep clean anyone else's path; you came here to walk your own.

Let go of what has served its purpose.

You will know if you are completely done with something when you give it up and you feel freedom instead of loss. This is when you will know that it is done serving its purpose in your life. The value has run out, the lesson has finished, and it's time to move on.

When you let go, you gain.

As you grow older you will let go a little at a time: a bad memory, a negative habit, a toxic friend. Bit by bit, you will shed what no longer serves you until you reveal who you are underneath it all. You will soon discover that even though you gave up many things, there is no feeling of loss. What you have gained in return is far more valuable.

Don't listen to the naysayers.

Some will come at you with criticism from the sidelines. Unless they're in the game with you, unless they're kicking up dirt and taking risks like you, consider them background noise. Keep your head where it's needed, focused on your goals. Let them do what they do best: criticize a game they're too afraid to play themselves.

Your power is in the present moment.

Your power is not in yesterday or in tomorrow. It's not over there somewhere waiting for you to reach it. It's not hidden behind some goal or achievement. Your power is right here, right now. Your power is within the choices you make today.

The average person makes 35,000 decisions a day. How many decisions did you make today that brought you closer to better health, to thriving relationships, a personal goal, or a happier life? Choose more of what benefits you and less of what keeps you in the same old unproductive and unhealthy cycles.

Peace is flowing with yourself, not against yourself.

True inner peace means all aspects of yourself are in harmony with each other. You're not using one part of yourself against another part of yourself. Your thoughts, feelings, intentions, and actions align with each other. You're not fighting, shaming, or abusing your inner workings; you're not in conflict with your process. Instead, you're in a state of inner allowing and harmony.

You're worth the effort.

Don't let anyone make you believe you're not worth the time and energy it takes to resolve a disagreement, listen to your thoughts, validate your feelings, or work on building a healthy relationship with you.

If you find yourself as the dominant initiator of interactions and communications, then you're going to start feeling as if you're the only one putting in the effort to keep the relationship going. If someone doesn't make the time for you, it's not because you don't deserve it. If they're unwilling to meet your efforts, they're not for you.

Relationships work best in balance, and anyone who doesn't want to give to you is not really in a relationship with you. They are simply taking advantage of an opportunity you keep providing for them. You give and they take until, eventually, you are left exhausted and unhappy.

The more unbalanced it gets, the more you'll feel it through your frustrations. You will then be faced with a choice: keep forcing something that isn't working or move onto someone who will meet your efforts with enthusiasm and love. Don't you deserve that?

Bad habits carry positive intentions.

You're not a bad person for having negative or harmful habits. We all have patterns that are unhealthy and unproductive. One day, we started doing it because it made us feel better; now, all it does is create problems. So when you realize that it's time to change a pattern, start with inquiry.

What is the positive intention behind the negative behavior? What are you really trying to accomplish with this habit? How can you satisfy that intention in a way that's more beneficial and less harmful?

Over-eating isn't about delicious food; it's about anxiety relief, suppressing anger we don't want to face, or emotional protection. You're not trying to harm yourself with food; you're trying to ease your pain. Once you understand the positive intention behind the negative behavior, you can then learn a healthier way to do it.

Don't let changing emotions run your relationships.

All relationships have emotional inconsistency. Don't expect to feel the same feeling all the time within your relationship. Your emotions will ebb and flow. You'll feel anger, happiness, sadness, joy, annoyance, excitement, etc. One day, you won't like your partner; and on other days, you'll love them very much. This is a normal process.

Don't assume that just because you're having a bad day that you have a bad relationship. Your emotions will color your thinking. Give yourself some time if you need it, and keep in mind that emotions shift and fluctuate. It's what they do. Don't let that ruin your relationships.

Learn to soothe yourself.

Find a soothing practice that helps calm and balance you. Whether it's meditation, yoga, or dance, practice it as often as you can so it becomes a habit. This will help you stay balanced during everyday stresses, and it'll help you return to balance when you feel overwhelmed or depressed. Consider it a mental first-aid kit. When you feel that stressful "cut," do your soothing practice to help it heal faster.

Let your emotions pass.

Feelings are sensations in the body. You don't have to fear them. You don't have to run from them or dismiss and ignore them. If you can stay with the sensation, it will soon pass. You don't have to attach a story to them or create meaning out of them. Simply let them be the knot in your stomach, the lump in your throat, the dizzying feeling on the top of your head. It's not a warning sign of something terrible happening. It's simply the anger, sadness, or frustration moving through your body. Let it pass through.

Get ready for another chance.

Just because you can't do something today, doesn't mean you can't do it tomorrow. You might be lacking an important understanding or a small piece of the bigger picture right now. That doesn't mean you can't learn it and become ready for tomorrow.

Don't give up on something simply because you're not ready for it in this moment. Instead, get ready. Keep doing the work. Use today to learn more and to understand what you need to understand. If you can't do it today, get ready for tomorrow.

Keep a journal.

Writing is a form of therapy, much like other methods of art. It allows you to release all of your feelings onto paper, where it can't hurt others. It also helps you understand your mental and emotional processes better. You can reread your writings and see it from a secondary viewpoint once you feel calmer. This will help you stay objective as you read about your experiences.

A journal can also help you get unstuck. You can view your problem from a clearer perspective and see what isn't working. You don't have to show your rants to anyone. Let the journal be a place for you to work out your inner processes. It doesn't have to be pretty; it just has to be honest.

Time management is really mind management.

If you can cut down on unproductive mental activities, you can save a lot of time. If you stop worrying about things you can't control, then you have more time to focus on things you can control. If you can remove your attention from what you can't do, what isn't working, who isn't complying and instead work on increasing what you can do, what is working, and who is supporting you, then you can spend some extra time learning new skills. You'll increase your productivity ten times by directing your attention on where you can be the most effective. It's not so much about adding more time; it's about using the time you have more efficiently.

Get comfortable with discomfort.

It's important to know the difference between not wanting to do something for a valid reason and not wanting to do it simply to avoid feeling uncomfortable. A lot of times, you'll decline an invitation not because you don't want to go, but because you want to prevent discomfort. If you continue to give into your need for avoidance, you'll stop your growth.

If you can push through discomfort, then you can enter the growth zone. This will help you learn new skills to cope with social situations that normally make you feel awkward. You learn through experience and practice, not avoidance. Your confidence will increase every time you step into the discomfort as opposed to running away from it.

Try some Mitzvah therapy.

Human beings are social creatures. We are wired to connect. So when we help others, we feel better about ourselves. We feel valuable, important, and empowered. We can see that we have made a difference in the world around us, and that enhances our self-worth.

Mitzvah therapy has been known to help with low self-esteem and depression. It also helps with feelings of isolation and powerlessness. You will begin to feel as though you matter because you mattered to the person you helped. You will start to feel confident in your power to effect change around you. So if you find yourself drowning in your negative thoughts, try to be of service to someone else.

Avoid the self-pity trap.

Our personal development is in direct proportion to the amount of responsibility we are willing to accept for our lives. The more we pity ourselves, the more we stunt our growth toward independence and healing. We might receive some comfort from others, but that won't change our circumstances in the long run.

Self-pity is not the same as self-compassion. Compassion leads us to understanding, recovery, and growth. Pity creates self-victimization and keeps you stuck in the same patterns. It doesn't change your life for the better. In fact, the more you pity yourself, the less you feel empowered enough to take the much-needed steps toward change.

Self-compassion is offering yourself love, kindness, and understanding so you can move forward and heal. Self-pity is disempowering, and it makes you feel miserable about yourself and your life. One embraces your power; the other takes it away.

Blame is disempowering.

In life, you will find many valid reasons to blame others for your experiences, feelings, and circumstances. And for the most part, you will be right. But that won't leave you in the position of power. You will be unable to change those circumstances because blame takes away your control over a situation. If it's another person's fault, then you become dependent on their corrective actions before you can move forward. You won't find peace without an apology or a rectification. The unfortunate fact is that you might never get either one.

Instead, you must decide that the other person's actions don't matter in how you proceed. You must take responsibility for your own life and turn it into something positive or productive for yourself regardless of how other people have behaved. If you continue to give them power over your emotions or your choices, then it's your life that will suffer the consequences. The fact is, you can't punish other people by destroying your own life.

Be a little selfish.

Healthy people are appropriately selfish. They know when it's time to take care of themselves and when it's time to give to others. They understand that crucial balance because without it, they wouldn't be healthy.

If you mostly give of yourself but don't recharge, you will deplete yourself into sickness. Then, you won't have any energy or health left to give to others. If you do that enough times, you will become chronically ill. Your desire to take care of others will backfire on you, and then others will have to take care of you.

Accept yourself, past and present.

Accepting yourself means accepting the past you, the present you, and who you are becoming. It means accepting the choices you have made with the understanding that you believed it was the right choice the moment you made it.

You are allowed to change your mind because you are allowed to grow. You are allowed to disagree with your past choices, but that's not the same as rejecting your past self. You don't have to agree with any of it, but to move on, you will have to accept it for what it was—a learning experience. Give yourself space and permission to learn.

Accept that you are doing the best you can in every moment. Even if this current learning moment has you sitting on the couch crying because you can't figure out your life. Maybe that's the best you can do right now. Don't judge yourself for it. One day's best won't look the same as another day's best. All that matters is that you accept yourself as you are today. Through that acceptance, you will open the doorway to appropriate change.

Let go when it's time.

Not everything you invest your energy into will reward you. Sometimes, you will find yourself in a relationship that is not balanced, you will find yourself in a friendship that isn't respectful to you, or you will find yourself at a job that isn't going anywhere. You have to know when it's time to walk away from something or someone that is no longer adding value in your life. You have to know when it's time to let go of the things that drain your energy, take up your time, or make you sick.

Practice turns an amateur into a professional.

Every single athlete has missed first before they hit a goal. Every single runner started off running poorly before they built up their stamina. Actors don't get every audition they go to, and singers can't hit all the right notes every time.

Regardless of how smart or talented you think you are, your dedication and continual practice of your craft is what will ultimately determine if you're great at it.

We all start off as amateurs. It's the people who keep practicing and learn from their mistakes who become masters at what they do. Everyone has to put in the work to get the results. Luck might get you the opportunity, but it's your practiced skills that will help you keep it.

It's okay to disappoint other people.

Odds are that you will disappoint others at some point in your life. Not everyone is going to like what you say, what you do, or the choices you must make. Not everyone is going to agree with your ideas, beliefs, or values. Does that mean you shouldn't choose what is right for you? Does that mean you shouldn't have opinions or express your ideas?

Anticipating and fearing other people's reactions can kill your freedom of expression, your spontaneity, and your authenticity. You will end up giving up your voice and freedom so that others stay comfortable around you. You will shrink to make others feel better. But that won't make you feel better. It won't benefit you, and it won't benefit them either.

People grow from outside of their comfort zones. No one grows from agreement and harmony. It's okay to challenge people. It's okay to disappoint them. It's okay to allow them the space to grow.

Don't let your emotions manage you.

The emotion itself is not unhealthy; it's the *expression* of the emotion that determines whether it is healthy or unhealthy. Anger doesn't hurt other people, and sadness doesn't change your life; it's the behavior from those emotions that does. Are you lashing out at others from anger? Are you destroying your relationship through your sadness? Then, it is an unhealthy expression.

It's not the emotion's fault—we all go through a wide range of emotions every day. However, not everyone makes life changes due to their temporary feelings. You must learn appropriate ways to express and manage your emotions, or else they'll run your entire life.

Betraying your integrity makes you weak.

If it doesn't feel right to you, say or do something about it. If you let go of an opportunity to do the right thing, you will feel it in the pit of your stomach. If it doesn't seem kind, don't do it. If you know you would rather stay home and get more sleep, say no to the offer to go out. If your boss crosses a personal line, speak up. Every time you miss of the chance to be authentic, your integrity suffers. And when your integrity suffers, you can feel it in your body.

You know when you've let yourself down. You know when you didn't do what was right. You know when you're lying. You know when you're giving into something you would rather not do. And every time you betray your authenticity, you will feel more and more of your empowerment drain. You will feel weaker because disempowerment makes you weary. To be strong, you have to stand in your integrity.

Speak well of yourself.

It's one thing to speak your truth or to share a story about your life; it's another thing to speak badly of yourself or to self-deprecate. Don't abuse yourself in front of others because you teach them how to treat you. You inadvertently give them permission to do the same thing to you. If you call yourself stupid in front of other people, it will teach them to call you stupid next time you make a mistake.

If you need to apologize for something, do it humbly. Admit your faults and wrongdoings. That's a sign of a mature adult, and it's honorable. However, don't call yourself insulting names as you do it. Your apology isn't superior simply because you beat yourself up while you did it. Belittling yourself doesn't help you learn or grow. It only keeps you small.

It's important to understand our weaknesses and to work on them, but that doesn't include putting ourselves down in front of others. Everyone is in the process of learning through experience. You're not the only one who feels incomplete or bad. That does not mean you *are* incomplete or bad.

Emotional independence is key.

No one is truly independent until they stop living for other people's approval, praise, respect, or pride. An adult is someone who makes their own decisions without trying to prove anything to anyone. Once you feel the need to prove something, then your life is no longer yours. It belongs to the person you are trying to win over, or show off to, or prove wrong.

Any time you make a choice because of another person's past, present, or possible future response, then they control your life, not you. Your life becomes a reaction to others, not a choice you consciously made that was grounded in your best interests. If you continue with the mentality of a child who lives off of the responses of others, then your life will never belong to you. Instead, those who have power over your emotions will dictate your direction and moods.

You become your influences.

Every song you hear, every movie you watch, every book you read will affect your mental or emotional state to some degree. In the same way that you consume either nutritious or junk food for your body, you also consume beneficial or wasteful information for your mind.

What you feed yourself will create an internal change in some way. The affect can be emotional, mental, chemical, biological, or spiritual. It will nourish your energy or drain it. It will add value to your life or harm it. It will change you for better or for worse.

We are receivers who take in information, energy, and experiences from all around us. The healthiest thing you can do is to become protective of who and what has access to your focus.

Everything in the world will compete for your attention. The Internet, TV, news, actors, musicians, parents, friends, co-workers—anyone you focus on has a potential influence on your thoughts, feelings, choices, and actions. Choose them wisely because over time you become more like your influencers.

Don't envy what you don't understand.

We never know the level of pain, sweat, or sacrifice that went into other people's accomplishments or successes. We don't know what they had to give up to end up where they are. We don't know the traumas they had to endure to learn their lessons, or the people they lost along the way. We didn't endure their depression or spend long nights talking them back into their goals when they almost gave up.

Success always looks easy and fun to those who didn't have to walk the path. You might not want the life they had to live to get to where they are now. What you're seeing is the end result, which feels enviable. However, don't envy the success, admire the strength and willpower it took to get there. Let it inspire you on your own journey.

Love your work or love why you work.

Work only feels like work when you don't want to do it. When you feel passionate and purposeful, you can work all day and still have energy left over after you get home. When you force yourself to do something you don't want to do, one hour can feel like ten.

Financial stability is important, but so is loving the work you do. You will spend most of your days away from your loved ones. You will spend more time at work than with your family. If you're going to sacrifice your time with them, make sure it's worth it. Make sure the work feels enjoyable, purposeful, and fulfilling or else you will feel cheated and drained.

However, if for whatever reason you can't work at something you love, know that there is no shame in doing convenient and available work in the meantime to provide for your family. If they're your reason *why* you work, then your work is purposeful nonetheless. It serves the purpose of providing for your loved ones, and there is honor in that. You won't always be where you want to be, so remember your "why" as you work toward your goals.

Challenges pave the way.

Sometimes, things don't work out the way we want them to and we are forced to improvise or settle for something we didn't want. Don't take this as a sign of failure. What might seem like a "no" now could actually be paving the way for a bigger "yes" later.

We can't ever see all the ways things are working out for us in the long run. What might seem like a detour right now might actually be the next step toward achieving our goals. That job you didn't want might lead you to the one you do. That "no" you received on a project might lead you to an even better "yes" with improved conditions you didn't know you wanted.

Everyone's success stories are filled with examples of circumstances that didn't work out but led them down what they now consider to be the right path.

We don't need to completely understand the shifting pieces and where they fit in our lives. All we have to do is just get through the current challenge in front of us and believe that it serves a bigger purpose in our lives.

All you need to do is take a step forward.

You can't always hold out for perfect timing or the right circumstances before you allow yourself to progress. Sometimes, you need to take what's available because it'll move you forward. It may not take you straight to your goal, but it might just move you closer to it.

You don't need big strides or giant leaps to feel as if you're succeeding. You just need to move in the general direction of where you want to be. Trust that the next steps will become clearer as you get closer.

What appears bad initially can be a blessing in disguise.

There will come a point in your life where you will believe that everything is falling apart around you. You will witness aspects of your life changing: relationships, jobs, income, health. It'll happen fast and it'll happen in multiple areas in your life.

You will wonder if anything will ever be the same again. It won't. But this is a good thing. Major life changes appear negative on the surface. However, once the dust settles and the pieces fall together, you will find that everything worked out exactly as it should.

Work smart, not hard.

Working hard isn't the same thing as being productive. You could be busy misplacing your energy into something that can't move forward. You can spend ten hours working, but only make real progress for ten minutes.

When you can prioritize your time accurately, you won't just become more efficient, you'll also be respecting your time and energy. You're not just filling your schedule with things to do. You're picking the actions that will maximize your efforts.

It's not so much about the time you invest as it is about spending your time wisely. We all get the same twenty-four hours in a day, but some people know how to use them more efficiently. Try to learn from their habits so you can do the most without giving the most.

Your time and energy are resources that you use through your focus. Don't exhaust them through unclear and misdirected actions. You don't have to work harder; you just need to work smarter by refining your focus.

Playing it safe is also a risk.

There are two risks in life: going for it, and not going for it. Most of the time, we think the true risk lies in taking the chance, so we try to play it safe by not going for it. However, sometimes not taking the risk is an even bigger risk because staying where we are isn't always the best decision.

Imagine if no one took a risk in moving out of their parents' house. Imagine if no one wanted to chance going to college or getting married or having children. Changing anything is a risk, whether it's relationships, jobs, cars, or housing. You risk one thing to gain another. If you value what you want more than what you have to give up, it won't feel like much of a risk.

There's only so much you can avoid risking before you cut yourself off from new experiences, growth, progress, and life in general. Every new experience is a gain in understanding, skill, and capability. Don't be too scared to take a risk every once in a while. Even if you lose, you gain.

Don't let people control you through their opinions.

Most of the time, we are offended because we have been taught to place more value on someone else's thoughts, feelings, and experiences than our own. We allow other people to shape our self-image so when they can't see or treat us the way we deserve to be seen or treated, we feel offended.

At some point, you're going to have to decide not to allow others to take your dignity through their opinions and expressions. Every time you are offended, you give a piece of your personal power away to the person who provokes you. With your anger, you're saying, "Your opinion of me matters more than my opinion of myself."

When you choose to get offended, you choose to get involved in their emotions and perceptions of you. Cut the emotional and mental cord from those who can't see you the way you deserve to be seen. They don't matter.

With the right people, you can do anything.

You can get to or get through anything in life with the right support system in place. Whether you are trying to get through a tragedy or build a dream, nothing is impossible with a good team of people.

Don't isolate yourself when you're embarking on a difficult task. Seek out those who can offer you what you need to lighten your load. We are social creatures that have survived unimaginable horrors throughout history because anything is made more bearable through the love and support we receive from others.

We have also made great strides in technology, medicine, and transportation because of teamwork. When the right people come together, magic happens. So unless you intend to break the laws of science, remember that anything is possible and made probable through a good support system.

Don't invest in other people's opinion of you.

You can change yourself a hundred different ways to get other people to approve of you and there will still be those who don't. Your beauty will please some and threaten others. Your intelligence will impress one person and offend another. You will be too tall, too short, too smart, too attractive, too nice, not nice enough, too talented, too poor, and not educated enough for people who are determined to not like you. You must decide that it doesn't matter what anyone else thinks of you. Their opinions don't make your bed, pay your bills, or fill your stomach, so stop investing your focus and energy into them.

Don't be in a rush to get it right.

The formula for success is easy. Be yourself, do what you love, learn from your mistakes, and don't give up. What they don't tell you is that it might take you 35 years to learn who you really are before you can be yourself. It might take you another 10 years to understand what you love doing. It might take an additional 15 years to apply all the lessons you've learned.

The formula is easy, but the execution takes time. Learning about yourself is a part of the process so don't think you're wasting time by engaging in trial-and-error experimentation. Understanding your weaknesses, strengths, limits, likes, dislikes, and where you thrive takes experience and time. It's valuable information that you need to succeed.

Don't be in a rush to get it right. Most of success is learning from getting it wrong. In the meantime, prepare for what you want to achieve. Read the right books, seek out the appropriate mentors, do your research, and take it step by step. Nothing is built overnight.

If you follow your own compass, you'll never get lost.

The future won't be better through a benevolent and wise leader; it can only be better through a benevolent and wise you. The greatest leader in the world won't be able to lead a people too unwise to see his greatness. Nothing changes without the will of the people.

In the same way, nothing in your life changes without the will of you. Your future depends on the choices you make every day. It depends on who you are becoming now. It depends on the books you read, the company you keep, and the mentors you choose. It's found through following your own internal compass and taking self-responsibility. It's built from intuition, trial-and-error, and an open mind. It's built from the inside out.

The world is full of people waiting for someone else to save or lead them. In this way, none of those people have actually grown up. True adulthood doesn't happen without self-leadership. You either choose your life or you spend your life waiting for the right someone to make the right choices for you.

Nobody else is within your control.

If you want to save yourself a lot of future pain and suffering, learn early what is yours and what is not. Not in regards to possessions or things, but in regards to what you have control over and what you don't.

Your emotions are yours. Other people's emotions are theirs. It sounds simple enough, and yet we spend most of our lives trying to change what isn't ours to change.

You must allow others to have their own growth experiences. This doesn't mean that you shouldn't offer them support or encouragement when they need it. It means you don't get to decide for others what they need. You are the only one within your control. And even you find it a hard process to manage yourself.

You don't need to compare yourself to motivate yourself.

*Should*ing on yourself doesn't motivate you. It doesn't trigger your passion, and it doesn't inspire actions that make you happy. It's our misguided attempt to pressure, manipulate, or guilt-trip ourselves into compliance.

Most of the *should*ing we do to ourselves is because we are comparing our lives to other people's lives. I should be settled. I should be married. I should have children. I should be at the height of my career. I should be wealthy.

Most of our *shoulds* go against our current reality. This is why we feel unhappy when we think about them. We are reminding ourselves of what we are missing. If you should be doing something, it means you're currently not doing it. Contrary to what we think, this is not motivating at all. Placing that kind of pressure on yourself won't activate your passion in life. It'll just keep you stuck and unmotivated. Maybe even depressed.

The only thing you should do is live your life on your natural timeline. Let your passions propel you forward otherwise your *should*s will act as anchors.

You don't have to change people if you choose wisely.

We all have potential to be great. We also have the potential to be unkind, unmotivated, and negative. All the good and bad things about a human being are possible within all human beings.

Some people are drawn to the negative ones, and they'll spend their whole lives struggling to heal, fix, and change them into something better. What they don't realize is that if you choose wisely, you don't need to change anyone.

You don't have to chase after a negative person who has the potential to be great. Instead, find someone motivated enough to change themselves. Find someone who is already on the path toward becoming a better person. They will continue to do the work, and you can support them along the way. That's the healthier alternative.

So get out of the business of changing people. You'll fail every time. Even doctors, priests, and therapists can't help those who don't want to help themselves. Don't waste your time, health, and energy on someone who would rather stay where they are.

You are not everyone's caretaker.

No one is allowed to dump their feelings all over you simply because they feel like it. Being a good friend is not the same as being a good punching bag. Don't allow others to drain your energy or release their negativity on you just because you care.

It's important to be a good friend, but if someone is taking advantage of your good nature, it might be time to let them go. They don't have the right to demand your time, attention, or energy just because they believe they should have access to it anytime they please. If they do that, then they're not a good friend for you.

You are no one's designated savior, counselor, or mother. You are not responsible for their emotional wellbeing. Don't put that kind of accountability on yourself because you'll fall short. You have to let other people find their own way. This is how we grow.

When you feel overwhelmed, take it step by step.

If you're having a difficult time or are feeling overwhelmed, stay in the present moment as much as you can and simply finish the task at hand. When you wake up in the morning, what's the first thing you would do? Go to the bathroom, brush your teeth, or take the dog out? Do that. Don't think about all the other things you need to do. Finish the task in front of you, then do the next task.

Stay with the present moment as you go through your day. Are you eating breakfast? Sit with your breakfast, feel the texture of your food, really taste it. Be mindful of the task in front of you. It doesn't matter if the task is "big" or "small"—it matters that you're doing it.

Don't think about tomorrow or the tasks that await you in the future. Just do the task in front of you now. Tomorrow will take care of itself.

People are doing the best they can.

Everyone wants relief. Whether it's the drug addict, the businessman, the thief, or the artist. There is no one who is not seeking relief from some kind of frustration, pain, or problem. The difference is that some people know how to find relief appropriately and others don't.

It's not so much that some people are bad and some people are good. It's that some people were raised with proper coping habits and others were not. It's not easy navigating this world when no one has taught you how to navigate your own thoughts and feelings.

How people act on the outside is an indication of how healthy they are internally. It's not your job to fix others, but it helps to understand them. For your own sake, try to remember that people are doing the best they can.

If you can keep this in mind, you'll understand why people do the things they do. It's rarely ever because they want to hurt someone else; it's mostly because they want relief for themselves.

Laugh as often as you can.

Life is so much harder when you take everything seriously. You create a wall to prevent more of the negative things from getting in. Unfortunately, the wall stops the good things as well. So you end up living your life protected, but unhappy.

Mostly, the wall of seriousness means you're afraid of being vulnerable. People don't realize this, but it takes courage to laugh. Laughter requires that you put your guard down to have a good time. It opens you up so you can enjoy the moment. You can't be happy while feeling tight, closed-off, and defensive. You must relax first.

When you're laughing, everything is okay for that one moment in time. It's not much, but it's enough to change your mood and help you enjoy your life.

Tell people the truth.

People deserve to know the truth. If you respect them, if you love them, then you must trust in their ability to handle their own reality. Whatever pain you think you're protecting them from is only temporary. It might also be necessary.

This might be an essential step in their growth or a life change that they desperately need. You don't want to keep that from them simply because you want to avoid delivering a painful message. Just because the message comes through a painful truth doesn't mean it's not right.

Trust that they are strong enough to get through the pain of knowing it. Support them through it, offer your help, but tell them either way. Our loved ones deserve the truth.

Everyone gets it wrong because that's how we learn.

One of our biggest fears is that we will be wrong about something or someone. Perhaps it's a life choice, a relationship, a job, or something even simpler than that, like an opinion. Sometimes, we are so afraid of getting it wrong that we don't even take the risk. We miss the opportunity to experience something we want because we doubt our judgment. When we do this, we miss the opportunity to grow from the experience.

What's so wrong about being wrong? You can change course when you realize it is not the appropriate choice for you. You can dump the wrong relationship, you can get out of the wrong job, you can make another choice, or change your opinion. Does it matter that you got it wrong?

The fact is that everyone gets it wrong. How else do we learn? In life, you will be wrong and you will get over it. If you can make peace with the first part, the second part will come faster.

Hold yourself accountable, even if others can't do the same for themselves.

It doesn't matter if others are truthful; it matters that we are truthful. It doesn't matter if others do the right thing; it matters that we do the right thing. We can look at other people's behavior and use that as an excuse to behave just as terribly, but we are the ones who will have to answer for ourselves.

Take responsibility for your part in the conflict. Hold yourself accountable for your part in perpetuating the problem. Nothing is ever 100% someone else's fault. We participate in our personal conflicts to some degree or else they wouldn't be our conflicts.

When you don't know what to do to move a conflict into resolution, think about where you were responsible and hold yourself accountable for that. Own up to your end of the disagreement. Even if people can't hold themselves accountable, you take the high road anyway. It doesn't matter what others do; it matters what you do. Your integrity is about you.

Know yourself to know what's right for you.

Life is a journey of self-discovery and self-creation. As you grow older and participate in a variety of experiences, you will discover aspects of yourself that you didn't know existed. Maybe there's some hidden jealousy, insecurity, or another weakness you weren't aware of. You will then get to decide whether you want to keep those aspects or change them. This is the self-creation process.

The fact is that you can't know what's right for you if you don't know who you are. One person's right is another person's wrong. You can't base your choices on other people's right choices. They may not be right for you.

You can't know what the right path, right relationship, or what the right career is if you don't have some experiences with the wrong ones. This is how you discover who you are and what you want to create for yourself.

If you want to help others, help yourself first.

A bountiful tree can feed many in one season. The tree doesn't stress itself trying to give its fruit away. It doesn't worry about not having enough for everybody. It doesn't run around looking for people and animals to feed. It simply nourishes itself, grows stronger, and becomes more abundant. Then, it gives to others.

The more you invest in yourself, the more you are able to help others. The more you give to yourself, the more you have to give to others. As the saying goes, you can't pour from an empty cup. You can't give what you don't have.

Nourish yourself through self-care, self-compassion, and self-responsibility. Consider these things sunshine and water. You need them to grow healthy and strong. When you replenish yourself, you can give to others again and again.

Discipline is a constant.

Know the difference between self-discipline and self-abuse. Pushing yourself to the point of mental, emotional, and physical exhaustion is not discipline. Neither is telling yourself that you are incompetent, unqualified, or a failure when something doesn't go as planned.

Discipline is about consistency and persistence. It's about self-motivation and continuous progress. Some days, you will make big strides; other days, you will take small steps. If you engage in self-abuse, then you will berate yourself for taking small steps instead of seeing how it all fits into the big picture. You will crush your motivation as opposed to feeding it. You will tell yourself it's not good enough or it's not big enough instead of appreciating any step forward.

Don't measure progress prematurely. It'll kill your momentum and motivation. Discipline says: do the work regardless of the speed and magnitude of the progress. If you show up every day and do what you need to do that day, then everything will take care of itself.

Invest yourself in a relationship with high returns.

If you're putting a lot of time, focus, and investment into a relationship that drains you, then it's not maintaining its value in your life. It's not adding to the quality of your life; instead, it's taking your good qualities and not reciprocating any of it back to you.

When you finish interacting with someone, do you feel energized or drained? Do you have more clarity, wisdom, and insight, or do you feel belittled and emotionally dumped on? Are you filled with possibilities or limitations? Do you feel lighter and freer, or are you more drained, frustrated, and insecure?

All relationships either feed you or drain you. The healthiest relationships will have a balance of give and take. You both offer something valuable to the other person, and you both leave the interaction feeling better about yourself and your circumstances.

Don't invest your energy into anyone who returns it at depreciated value. What you're receiving from the other person should be as significant as what you're giving.

Sometimes, a fresh perspective is all you need.

Just because you're obsessing about a problem doesn't mean you're working it out. Time spent on an issue doesn't equal time spent on a solution. You could be going in circles and not seeing something important that could change the way you experience it.

A fresh mind with a different perspective can offer you more in a few minutes than all the days you spent ruminating over it in your own mind. Consider advice from multiple people, but always go with what you feel is right.

Important messages require good timing.

Sometimes, you'll hear or read a message that doesn't quite feel appropriate in your current life situation. Don't dismiss the message as wrong. It still contains wisdom. It just might not be what you need as this moment. A message that is wrong in one situation might be right in another.

Keep it in mind and come back to it at another time. Sometimes, we're not ready to hear what's being said and we need to go through other experiences before we can take in the value of the message.

Everyone is your teacher; everything is a lesson.

You don't have to wait until you know everything before you can teach others. We are all students and teachers at the same time. We learn from one experience as we help or support others in their own experiences.

We can learn through books, courses, seminars, workshops, and retreats. We can learn from teachers, instructors, mentors, authors, and coaches. These are common forms of learning and teaching.

However, we also learn through divorces, car accidents, changing jobs, losing a project, and failing at a task. We learn from our spouses, children, friends, acquaintances, co-workers, and strangers. Our daily lives offer us lessons and teachers whether we realize it or not.

Everything you learn and experience now will become teaching tools that you can use to help others later. As you learn yourself, you become a better teacher for others.

Give to yourself first.

To everything, there is a season. Some seasons, you will give fruit; other seasons, you will need to rest and recover. The bare tree is not a failure. It is simply in the replenishment part of its cycle. That's a necessary part of its process because without it, the tree can't grow more fruit.

You don't have to give every time. It's okay for you to take some time for yourself, as well. In fact, if you want to have enough to give to others, you will need to take care of yourself first. A tree that refuses water and sunlight for itself can't bear fruit for others.

You must learn it to know it.

When you judge another person for their feelings or experiences, it's because on some level you believe that you are wiser. You believe you wouldn't have made their mistake because the answer seems so obvious to you.

Perhaps you wouldn't have made their mistake, but you are not living their life. It's possible that if you lived all that they have lived, you would make the same choices. It's simpler to see how "easy" a decision is when you have already learned those lessons. Perhaps from their perspective, it's not easy or obvious because they're still in the middle of the lesson.

There are many lessons you have yet to learn, as well. To others, it's so easy and obvious that they don't understand why you can't see it. What one person finds frustrating, another finds easy. What appears as difficult to understand for one is common sense for another.

Don't judge other people for where they are in life. Don't judge them for what they don't know. They're in the process of learning. Be kind to them in the same way you would want others to be kind to you while you're learning.

This world would not be the same without you.

You bring something special into this world with your distinctive experiences and thoughts. No one else has lived your life exactly as you have. No one else has ever had the same combination of events, circumstances, and life history as you. There is no one else like you.

What you bring to the world, no one else can. Your value is beyond compare, even if you don't realize it yet. So I hope you remember how important you are on days when you feel unworthy or insecure. I hope you remember that there is only one you and that we would all lose something priceless and irreplaceable without you.

You must be willing, or it won't work.

Some people can offer you guidance, while others can influence you. Some can help you move forward, while others can support you. Some will hold your hand, while others will walk with you.

However, no one can learn for you. No one can act for you. No one can walk your path for you. It doesn't matter how much guidance is offered if you don't take it. It doesn't matter how much help or support is given if you don't take it.

No one can help a person who doesn't want to be helped. No one can save a person who doesn't want to be saved. No one can change a person who doesn't want to be changed. You must be willing to do the work if you want to see the results.

Change your response, not the other person.

You can't change anyone else's behavior, especially if they're not willing to change it themselves. However, you can change the way you respond and interact with them.

You can't choose who another person is, but you can choose who you want to associate with. You can choose who you want to befriend, who you want to date, who you want to work for. You can't control others, but you can control your choices and responses to them. It's far easier to choose kind people than to choose an unkind person and try to change them into a kind person.

Understanding is key.

Don't worry so much about being right in a situation; care more about understanding it. The person who understands can lead everyone else into a resolution, while the person who wants to be right just ends up escalating the problem and separating themselves from the solution.

The person who wants to understand finds what is right, while the person who wants to be right can't understand. Focus on solutions, not sides.

Life is as big or as small as your courage.

It doesn't matter how lucky you think you are. It doesn't matter how much money you have, how vibrant you feel, or how many opportunities surround you. None of it matters if you don't have the courage to step into it.

The world is full of fun experiences; do you have the courage to go? It's full of smart people; do you have the courage to talk to them? It's full of wealthy people; do you have the courage to present your ideas and projects? It's full of gorgeous people; do you have the courage to ask them on a date?

You won't know where any path will lead if you don't have the courage to take it. Of course you'll hear some no's along the way, but the people who choose the big life don't let that stop them. It doesn't matter if the road is blocked—there's another one. It doesn't matter if one person rejects you—there's another one. What matters is that you choose to move forward with courage. Choose the big life; it's the only one worthy of your big dreams and your big heart.

It's okay to let it go.

There will come a time when you will try every which way to make something happen. You will give it your absolute best. You will try every avenue. You will do everything in your power, and it still won't work. When this occurs, know that it's okay to let it go.

You don't want to be stuck forcing something that won't happen. You'll waste your time, energy, and health on something that simply isn't meant for you. It's okay to move on. It's imperative that you move on. If you don't, you'll prevent even better things from coming into your life.

Not everything we want or strive for is meant to work out. Sometimes it's meant to teach us a valuable skill or lesson so we can use it somewhere else. Some experiences are only for growth purposes.

Learn what there is to learn, take the value of the experience, and let it go. As long as you tried your best, it's okay to stop. Quitting doesn't mean you failed. It means you're smart enough to recognize when something isn't working. Let it go so something better can take its place.

Don't place your partner on the opposite side.

An argument is not between two people. It's between two thought processes, two habits of behavior, two intentions, and two agendas. It wavers between understanding and misunderstanding, communicating and miscommunicating.

The problem is not so much your partner; the problem is the misunderstanding between you and your partner. You don't need to argue the other person into defeat or resignation. If you do that, no one wins.

Instead, think of it as you and your partner versus the problem, as apposed to you versus your partner. Work together to resolve your issues by creating a common goal. Don't make the other person the enemy. You won't want to listen or cooperate with them.

In a relationship, you have chosen to come together and share your experiences. So share them. Don't battle each other to see who has the valid experience. In doing that, you'll only negate the other person's feelings and experiences. Once you go down that road, your relationship is headed for eventual separation.

Thank you for sharing your truth.

I'm proud of you for speaking your truth. I know it must have been hard for you to be open and vulnerable about the way you feel. I know it was difficult to be honest about an experience they don't understand. I know it took a lot of courage for you to do it.

Thank you for sharing a part of yourself with us. Thank you for stepping into your truth. Thank you for opening yourself up so that others can learn and grow through your experiences. Thank you for being you. Your bravery is not only admirable, but also inspiring.

You're a kind and gentle soul.

I know that sometimes it feels as if the world doesn't understand you. You try so hard to be there for others. To make them feel supported and understood. You want so much for everyone to feel something you don't feel. You want them to feel like they belong. You want them to be heard and validated. You want them to feel special.

I want you to know that I see what a kind and gentle soul you are. I see how you never pass up an opportunity to make another person feel worth the time and effort. I want you to know that you are worth the time and effort, too. You are special, too. And even though it doesn't feel like it sometimes, know that there is someone in the world who knows just how amazing you are and loves you for it.

Most fear is useless.

Most of what you're afraid of is never going to happen. Your brain is programmed to watch out for negative events and circumstances as an automatic survival mechanism. This also includes trying to predict future harmful events and circumstances so you can avoid them.

The fact is you won't know what's going to happen until you do it. Your guess for a positive outcome instead of a negative one is just as possible. Most of what you'll attempt to accomplish will not be dangerous or life threatening, so in all likelihood it'll be a positive outcome or a neutral one.

Acknowledge the fear but move forward anyway because you can't let fear stop you from living your life. Most of the bad things that happen to us exist more in our imagination than in our reality.

Your life is happening right now.

If you wait for a certain accomplishment or milestone before you start living your life, your life will pass you by. The present is happening right now and it won't pause for you to lose weight or get a better job. The days, months, and years will pass as you wait for better circumstances before you can start enjoying your life.

It's important to plan for tomorrow, but it's also important to enjoy today. All you'll ever experience is today. Each today will move you forward into tomorrow, but you'll only ever experience it as today.

Your life doesn't begin after you graduate, after you get married, or after you get that job. It's happening this instant. If you keep putting it off, you'll waste away your years and then wonder where they went.

Trying to be someone you're not is a waste of energy.

If you try to be someone you're not, people will be able to see through it. In the same way that you are able to tell when others aren't being their authentic selves, they can tell when you're pretending, as well. You won't feel real and they'll be able to sense your pretense.

It takes more energy to maintain a false self-image or fake persona than to just be yourself. It's exhausting to hold onto someone else's energy and pass it off as your own. If you want to be light and free, you have to flow as yourself.

You can and you will get through it.

You can handle anything, even the things you think you can't handle. You're a lot stronger and wiser than you understand right now. You are capable of getting past your worst days.

Trust that you have what it takes to move through this. Just when you least expect it, you'll be able to reach down inside yourself and pull out a hidden strength you didn't know existed. You'll surprise yourself as you mature through the experience.

Whatever you're going through now, it's not bigger than you or your ability to grow into your strength. Human beings have survived some of the most unimaginable horrors possible. So, whatever it is you think you can't handle in your life, you can and you will.

Appreciation magnifies happiness.

Appreciating what you currently have in your life will magnify your happiness tenfold. The more you appreciate, the happier you'll become. Not only that, but whatever you appreciate will also multiply in your life. Gratitude brings more things to be grateful about.

You know the saying, "You can't buy happiness"? It's not so much that you can't buy things that make you feel happy, it's that if you don't appreciate the things you have, buying more of it will not bring you more happiness.

You will take pleasure in the thing for a short time and then grow tired and bored of it. Then, you'll simply move onto the next thing you think will fulfill you. Soon after, you'll take that for granted, too. The determining factor for your satisfaction is not what you have, but whether you appreciate it.

It's okay to be unlikable.

Most people will not like some aspect of you. You won't like some aspect of them. This is a normal occurrence that happens between people. It happens to everyone, and it happens every day. You are not for everybody. Everybody is not for you.

Don't expect everyone you meet to enjoy your company or want to be around you. Also, when you meet these people, don't hold onto them. Don't try to change their minds. Don't try to win them over by hiding or changing parts of yourself. It's normal that they don't want you. Not everyone will want you.

If someone doesn't like you, the world will not end. Let them not like you. Be unlikable. It's okay. Decide that no one else's opinion will uplift you or deflate you. All that matters is what you think of you.

Self-talk determines happiness and success.

Your self-talk can motivate you or drain you. It can inspire you or depress you. It can move you forward or hold you back. It might not construct your circumstances, but it helps you interpret, understand, respond to, and move past your circumstances.

The determining factor for our success and happiness is not our situation or other people; it's what we tell ourselves about these things. It's how we perceive and how we proceed.

Imagine you are placing a bet on a person's likelihood to succeed. You have to choose between two people from the same circumstances, same neighborhood, and same history. The only difference between them is that one believes their circumstances won't allow them to succeed and the other believes in their ability to overcome anything.

Who would you bet on? Who do you think is more likely to succeed? The one who believes he's limited and held back, or the one who's determined to succeed anyway? Positive self-talk will help you through any limitation, while negative self-talk *is* the limitation.

Self-love is healing.

Your heart is hungry for your own understanding. It yearns to quench its thirst for unconditional love through your compassion and acceptance. It craves for an authentic love that can't be taken away by words or actions. It needs a soul-shaking, mind-bending, heart-healing kind of love. The kind of love that no one and nothing else can break.

When you love yourself, it is always reciprocated. It is a full and complete love that is whole by itself. It doesn't require another heart, another soul, or another body. What it needs, it already has. It can be enhanced by another's love, but is complete onto itself. It is full. It is happy. It is healing.

Expand your mind as often as possible.

Read books by people you disagree with. Listen to others who think differently from you. Watch programming you normally wouldn't watch. Expand your mind and views of the world. As right as you think you are about your own beliefs and experiences, others feel the same way about their own. You'll learn more than you ever imagined if you see the world through beliefs rather than right and wrong.

Be on your own team.

The kind of life you have will depend on whether you fight *with* yourself or *for* yourself. If you spend most of your energy struggling with your own thoughts and emotions, then you won't have any left over for the obstacles on the path to your dreams. You'll give up easily because you'll be exhausted. You won't have any more fight in you because you will have inadvertently defeated yourself.

Naysayers don't know your calling.

People who advise you to be realistic are only talking about their real. Your real is different. What you want to do is probably far more realistic in your world than in theirs. You can't judge your life from other people's limitations. You can't live your life the way they live theirs.

We all have different roads, opportunities, and possibilities. If the idea came to you on your road, then it has a possibility of becoming real for you. If they don't get it, then they can't be a part of it, but that doesn't mean it won't happen for you.

You are uniquely beautiful.

You don't have to be anyone else's idea of pretty. You don't have to change anything to become more pleasing to someone else's eyes. You don't exist to make others comfortable with your beauty. It's not your job to be desired by others.

When you do what you love, when you wear what you enjoy, when you feel comfortable in your own skin, your confidence will make you radiate, regardless of what you wear or look like. Self-acceptance makes us uniquely beautiful.

You teach people how to treat you.

People will treat you as good or as bad as you allow them to treat you. If you allow bad behavior to continue, it will. If you allow them to disrespect you, they will. If you allow them to walk all over you and then blame you for their feelings, they will.

People will try to get away with all kinds of terrible behavior. They won't stop it simply because they love you. They'll only stop it if you stand up for yourself.

Don't be afraid to let people know when they cross your boundaries or behave disrespectfully. If they are going to be in your life, then they must take responsibility for their own behavior. If they are unable to do that, then you won't be able to maintain a healthy relationship with them.

You're allowed to think for yourself.

It's okay if you don't agree with someone. It's okay if they don't agree with you. You're allowed to think, feel, and believe differently from others. They are allowed the same right as well.

Seven billion people are not going to agree with each other. People have their own set of beliefs for how and why they came into this world. They have their own set of values and ethics. They have their own understanding for proper conduct and behavior.

Don't let other people convince you that you shouldn't have an opinion simply because it doesn't match theirs. Don't be afraid to speak freely. Don't be afraid to share your thoughts. You can't regulate or control other people's thinking, and you can't allow others to regulate or control yours either.

Appreciate your parents' wisdom.

When your parents offer you advice, know that they're giving you the best of what they have learned. They picked it up through decades of pain, heartache, and hard lessons. They are offering it to you to save you the trouble of having to go through what they went through.

You might decide that the advice is not right for you. It might not apply to your situation. You might be living a different experience or life. It's even possible you won't need that advice. Either way, know that it comes from a place of deep love and concern. So even if you don't take the advice, appreciate the intention behind it.

Give people space to be happy.

Most people want the same things in life. They simply define them through different expressions and means. We all want to be happy and healthy. But that might look differently with different people. If you want to understand your partner better, understand their definition of happiness and how it's expressed in their lives. Then, give them room to be happy.

Is happiness freedom, security, or service and contribution? Is it a sense of accomplishment? How does it show up? Does freedom show up as time spent fishing alone? Does service and contribution show up through fixing things around the house? Does a sense of accomplishment show up as checking everything off the to-do list?

Whatever it is, however small it is, acknowledge it when it happens. Just because it doesn't look like your definition of happiness doesn't mean it's not exactly what the other person needs or enjoys doing. Let them have their moment. Give them the time to themselves. Let them have instances of happiness, even if it's without you. This will help your relationship thrive.

Getting together is easy; staying together takes work.

A friendship or relationship happens when two people are pulled together naturally through mutual attraction. The attraction can be a physical one, an energetic one, or both. Either way, once the connection has been made and both people choose to participate in a relationship, it takes a bit of work to keep it together.

It takes being open and honest, even on the days when it would be easier to hide or lie. It takes clear communication, even when you would rather play games or stay silent. It takes integrity, even when you would rather not be yourself sometimes. It takes mutual love, mutual respect, and mutual understanding.

If you can't or don't want to do the work, your relationship becomes vulnerable to termination. At that point, it's only a matter of who will get tired of all the games, lies, miscommunications, misunderstandings, and inauthenticity first. The further you step away from the core of your relationship, the closer you get to its end.

Grow your skillset.

When you invest in your own education and growth, it'll always be there for you to utilize when you need it. It's better to grow your own skills, talents, and knowledge than to rely on others for theirs. Sometimes, you will need the help of others, but be sure to learn what they do and how they do it so you can do it as well.

Don't just rely on others to give you what you need. You'll have to wait for them to decide when they want to help or under which conditions they're willing to do it. You'll become dependent on their moods, whims, and preferences.

It's better to trust and invest in yourself than to place your hopes and dreams on another person. Accept help, but learn from others as they're helping you. Don't be afraid to try it out, take the risk, learn the lesson, and expand your knowledge. Grow your skillset so you become indispensable.

Don't let others control you through their anger.

Some people will suck the life out of you by being constantly upset and angry with you. They'll demand that you explain yourself, they'll force you to defend yourself, they'll shame you, they'll manipulate you through guilt, and then they'll get you to apologize for it.

By the time you're finished interacting with them, they will have taken your energy, dignity, and whatever ounce of self-esteem you had left. They'll take you apart bit by bit, and you won't even notice until it's too late.

They'll become hurt and offended over the smallest things simply to control you. They'll use your good heart against you to gain dominance over you. And because you have a good heart, you'll let them. They'll convince you that you were wrong by making everything about their feelings.

You must take your energy and power back from these people. You must not let them control you through their constant victimization of themselves. The more you stay, the more they'll take from you until you're completely drained and questioning your understanding of yourself.

Healing can't be rushed.

Everyone heals in their own way and on their own timetable. It doesn't matter if the wound is physical, emotional, mental, or spiritual, healing can't be rushed or forced. It can't be dictated or controlled by another person. It doesn't have to look like anyone else's process. It doesn't have to be on their schedule or through their conditions.

Others can support us during the process. They can guide us through it. They can even influence our healing, but ultimately, the healing must happen on its own terms.

Give yourself the time you need to heal properly and thoroughly. Don't rush the process, or else you'll create the opposite effect. You'll make yourself stressed and frustrated, and this will slow down the process. Exercise self-compassion, self-love, self-forgiveness, and self-care to boost healing and to ensure that what you heal stays healed.

You got this.

When a problem shows up for you, you have to show up for the problem. That means you don't try to ignore it, dismiss it, or numb it away through addictions. If it's your problem, then you hold the power within you to solve it. You might have to grow a bit to do it, but you can do it. Be brave enough to acknowledge the problem and confident enough to know that no problem stands a chance when you show up.

If you believed in yourself more, you would fear less.

Most of what we're afraid of in life is our own feelings. We are rarely afraid of an actual event or thing. We are usually afraid of the feelings the event will trigger within us. We don't want to feel the stress, the helplessness, the frustration again. We don't want to become depressed again, we don't want to feel useless or out of control.

We don't know what to do with these emotions, and so we want to avoid triggering them. We avoid people, places, and situations that elicit emotions we don't know how to manage. We change up our whole lives because we are afraid to feel certain things.

If you had the ability to handle the event with confidence, grace, and keep your self-esteem in tact, you wouldn't fear it. You would handle it with ease. You would believe in your ability to handle anything, and your fear would subside.

If you want to increase your ability to handle events, you have to increase your ability to handle your emotions. You have to learn how to manage yourself, not anyone or anything else.

Don't rush things that need time to grow.

Everything won't be ready for you the moment you want it. Also, you might not be ready for it the moment you want it. You don't know all the ways in which your life will have to change for you to receive what you desire. Perhaps, right now, under these current circumstances, it would cause more harm than good.

Some things need time to grow into a better match for you. You might need time to grow into a better match for it. Maybe you can't handle that right now. Maybe you have more learning to do. You don't know what will be required of you and, therefore, you don't know if your desire is a match to who you are in this moment.

Circumstances might need time to shift before the right pieces fall into place. People might need more time to change their minds. You might need more time to grow. Issues might need time to resolve on their own. Don't try to rush something simply because you want it now. Getting it now might mean getting a version that won't work or one that won't make you happy.

Giving it a few days gives you a better perspective.

Try not to make big decisions through intense emotions. Give yourself some time to come back from the anger, sadness, frustration, or the euphoria, elation, and excitement before making important choices. What you choose might only be a result of how you feel in that moment. You could very well change your mind in a few days when you feel more stable.

If you still agree with your idea after you have returned to your baseline feelings, then you can pursue the choice more rationally. Giving it a few days will offer you more perspective, and it will help you make a better decision.

A lot of times, intense emotions make us feel as if it's an urgent matter and we must decide now. The emotion amplifies stress and fogs up our ability to think clearly. We might not realize that it's not workable or right for us until we think about it more logically. Give it some time so you are clear about what you want.

Some events are blessings, regardless of how bad they seem.

Every so often, you'll need to reflect on certain areas of your life. You'll have to review what's working and what isn't working so you can create a better life for yourself. However, most of us don't do that. We become so busy that we forget to check in with ourselves. We forget to ask ourselves if we are truly happy.

It's possible to become so used to things not working for so long that it becomes our normal. We don't notice how bad it has become until it gets worse. Usually, an event will occur that will force our eyes open. The event won't create the issue; it will only amplify the issue so we can't ignore it any longer. Then, we will be forced to make the changes that are necessary for our happiness.

During the process, we'll blame the event and anyone involved in it. We'll curse our luck or think it's because we did something wrong. We'll become wrapped up in our own insecurities and shame. But in hindsight, we'll see that it was exactly what we needed to see clearly.

Love means working on your relationship.

According to biology, it takes between 9-24 months before the euphoric effects of love begin to fade. You will know if you truly love someone after about two years. Anything before that is simply a chemical reaction fueled by attraction and hormones. It will make you blind to the flaws, annoyances, and idiosyncrasies of the other person.

It's usually after this period that couples experience major conflicts. They begin to see their partners more realistically, and they begin to weigh the pros and cons of the relationship. Once the high wears off, you will know if the love is real.

Are you willing to work through the conflicts even when the excitement is over? Are you willing to communicate openly and listen to some things you might not want to hear? Are you willing to accept the other person even when they're cranky, annoying, or stubborn? Do you want to stay with them because you genuinely enjoy their company? Are you in it long term, through the ups and downs, even when you don't feel like it sometimes? That's love.

Self-awareness is a form of self-education.

No real change can happen without self-awareness. If changes are made without awareness, it's because of an unconscious reaction. They are default changes that happen automatically because external events trigger internal responses.

However, if you are self-aware, you can observe yourself and apply changes where you feel they are necessary. You can take a neutral stance to observe your thoughts, behaviors, actions, and emotions before applying an appropriate response. This is pivotal for emotional independence. Otherwise, you are like an emotional pinball being knocked around from one side to another based on the moods of other people.

Self-awareness is a form of self-education. You begin to understand yourself through observing yourself. And as you understand yourself and why you think, feel, and behave as you do, you have power over your patterns and habits.

Self-acceptance is a respect for your personal reality.

Acceptance is a willingness to experience something without denial or avoidance. It's a form of openness that signifies a respect for your own reality and experience. Self-denial, comparison, and shame are self-disrespect. They signify a reluctance for self-acceptance.

If you experience something within yourself, don't deny it even if you dislike the feeling it has triggered. You think what you think. You feel what you feel. You are what you are. We must acknowledge and admit pieces and parts of ourselves to ourselves if we are to grow from them. You can't change what you don't acknowledge.

First, you must accept it as it is, then you can journey into understanding why and how it occurred. It's only after that exploration that you can change any part of it.

Saying no is a form of self-respect.

Respecting yourself also means respecting your own time and energy. It means saying no to energy-draining activities and people. It means not wasting your time on relationships that take from you but don't replenish you. It's about saying no to anything that doesn't offer you balance.

Be yourself, but allow space for growth.

Choose someone who you feel comfortable enough around to be yourself, but also choose someone who challenges you enough to help you grow. You don't want all comfort or all challenges because one will keep you stagnant and the other will exhaust you.

"How" solves problems faster than "why".

When working through a problem, think in terms of *how*, not *why*. Why leads to excuses, justifications, and blame. It can keep you stuck within a problem. How moves you forward into solutions. "How can I move past this?" is much more powerful than, "Why did this happen?" You might never know the answer to *why*, but you can find multiple *how*'s to move you through it.

Focusing on outcomes instead of problems takes you toward results. Focusing on problems leads you to find blame and limits. Outcome thinking keeps you open to solutions. Problem thinking keeps you stuck in the problem.

Enjoy today; it's all you have.

We wait for tomorrow, we wait for the weekend, we wait for a vacation, and before we know it, a year has passed. Without realizing it, we waste away our years waiting for another day to arrive. A day we get to celebrate, or enjoy, or be happy about. However, once it comes, we wait for another date, another event, or another occasion. We spend more time passing time than enjoying it. One day, you'll wake up and realize that you're much older than you thought you were, and you didn't enjoy as much as you could have. So, enjoy today because it's all you have.

The formula for success includes failure.

The biggest lie about success is that its opposite is failure. This tricks you into thinking that you're far away from your achievement or goal if things don't work out exactly as you wanted them to. However, there is no success without risk, experimentation, and some failure.

Disappointments, delays, and disasters are not contrary to success; they are a part of the process. If you experience failure, it doesn't mean you are on the other end of success. It means you're right on track as long as you don't give up. The opposite of success is resignation, not failure. You can't succeed if you give up, but you can succeed after you fail.

Acting through fear increases self-esteem.

Most fear exists before you act. It rises when you're just standing around thinking too much about what could happen instead of taking action. This keeps you immobile and anxious. However, once you take the step, once you jump off the cliff, then you're no longer afraid.

Fear converts into excitement, and this helps you gain more courage and confidence for next time. If you can get past your initial fear and take the leap, the fear will disappear and transform into more self-esteem.

Success means different things to different people.

Your progress might not look like other people's progress, which means your markers for success might be different as well. One person's success might involve getting a diploma, while another's might involve overcoming depression. Challenges come in different forms for different people, therefore success is different, too.

You're not failing in life simply because your life doesn't resemble someone else's. If you're slaying your own demons, then know that is the bravest and hardest thing any human can do. You shouldn't dismiss your challenges because someone else is doing something different elsewhere. Some people's battles involve conquering the business world, while other people's battles are within their own minds.

Their diplomas, jobs, and relationships shouldn't be compared to you fighting to establish your own inner harmony and health. Your work is not to get your life to look like anyone else's. Your work is to create the life that's meant for you through overcoming your own obstacles.

You are a verb.

You are not an entity who simply exists; you are a process that is continuously occurring. You think, you feel, you grow, you change, you function, you occur. You are happening. You are a verb.

You are a function of bodily, energetic, and intellectual systems that move, flow and process at every moment. Your body and brain alone are nothing without their procedures, methods, and functions. Otherwise, they're just inoperable clumps of organic matter with no use.

We use labels to stabilize our continuous flow and anchor ourselves to an identity. Instead of seeing ourselves as an ever-changing process, we see ourselves as a mother, brother, doctor, or teacher. This helps us mentally contain the magnitude of our actuality.

One of our functions includes our mind's ability to string together a continuity of moments that have occurred before and use that to create meaning for present experiences. It also uses our labels and identities as a filter for the present moment. This helps us understand our lives and experiences better.

It's important to remember this process because you as a

self go through multiple changes monthly, weekly, daily and even moment-to-moment. If a change doesn't feel consistent with our understanding of self, we think something has gone wrong. We forget that even that change can change again in a moment's notice. We prefer stability and consistency because it's simply easier to understand. However, this expectation causes suffering because we forget our true nature.

Labels link you to a personality, the past anchors you to meaning, and love attaches you to people and places. All of this comes together to create your self-image and self-understanding. However, your self is not a thing that you can step back from and understand. Your self is the process of understanding. You are a verb. You are not a self; you are *selfing.*

I have always been blessed,
though I didn't always know it.

I have always been loved,
though I didn't always believe it.

I have always been fortunate,
though I didn't always see it.

I have always been guided,
though it took me a long time to follow it.

The same is true for you,
though I hope you understand it now.

Thank You

I hope you've enjoyed my passages of wisdom and encouragement. I hope you were able to receive something valuable from this book.

You might also like my book **Thirty**, which contains over 230 of my personal quotes, lessons, and advice that I wrote in my thirtieth year. The four passages from pages 116-119 were taken from Thirty and used here with mild changes.

You might also enjoy **The Energy of Emotions, The Book of Relief,** and **The Empowered Self.** They are self-help books written with the intention of supporting the reader through self-understanding, self-growth, and self-healing.

My other books, **A Second Opinion, The Process of I**, and **Adventures in Thinking** are philosophical books intended to open the mind of the reader and awaken their consciousness to false beliefs, limited thinking, and harmful viewpoints.

Whether you want to explore your mind, your feelings, or your life, there's a book that can accompany you through the journey. Thank you again for choosing one of my books to expand your mind or to better your life experience.

About The Author

Emily Maroutian is an award-winning writer, poet, and philosopher. In 2009, she formed Maroutian Entertainment, a multimedia company that produces empowering material in the form of books, courses, movies, and TV shows.

She has been studying philosophy and personal development for more than a decade and combines her experiences from both fields in her works. She has written several books, including her 2015 metaphysical release, The Energy of Emotions, which became an Amazon.com bestseller.

Her other notable book, The Book of Relief, won the 2017 Bronze medal in the 9th annual Living Now Book Awards for Meditation/Relaxation. The awards are designed to honor the year's best books that help readers attain healthier, more fulfilling, and productive lives.

She has a notable ability of simplifying complicated philosophical concepts and turning them into useful resources for self-development. The focus of her work is to reframe common understandings to encourage personal transformation. Her philosophies center on the idea that we all have the power to better the world through bettering ourselves.

Made in the USA
San Bernardino, CA
10 September 2019